erotic poems

erotic poems

E. E. Cummings

Edited by
George James Firmage

W. W. NORTON & COMPANY
NEW YORK   LONDON

For information about permission to reproduce
selections from this book,
write to Permissions, W. W. Norton & Company, Inc.,
500 Fifth Avenue, New York, NY 10110

For information about special discounts for bulk purchases,
please contact W. W. Norton Special Sales at
specialsales@wwnorton.com or 800-233-4830

Manufacturing by The Maple Press
Book design by Lovedog Studio
Production manager: Anna Oler

Library of Congress Cataloging-in-Publication Data

Cummings, E. E. (Edward Estlin), 1894–1962.
Erotic poems / E.E. Cummings ; edited
by George James Firmage. — 1st ed.
p. cm.
ISBN 978-0-87140-659-0 (pbk.)
1. Erotic poetry, American. I. Firmage, George James. II. Title.
PS3505.U334E76 2010
811'.52—dc22
2009039886

W. W. Norton & Company, Inc.
500 Fifth Avenue, New York, N.Y. 10110
www.wwnorton.com

W. W. Norton & Company Ltd.
Castle House, 75/76 Wells Street, London W1T 3QT

1 2 3 4 5 6 7 8 9 0

erotic poems

iii.

there is a
moon sole
in the blue
night

     amorous of waters
tremulous,
blinded with silence the
undulous heaven yearns where

in tense starlessness
anoint with ardor
the yellow lover

stands in the dumb dark
svelte
and
urgent

     (again
love i slowly
gather
of thy languorous mouth the

thrilling
flower)

between the breasts
of bestial
Marj lie large
men who praise

Marj's cleancornered strokable
body   these men's
fingers toss trunks
shuffle sacks spin kegs they

curl
loving
around
beers

    the world has
these men's hands but their
bodies big and boozing
belong to

Marj
the greenslim purse of whose
face opens
on a fatgold

grin
hooray

hoorah for the large
men who lie

between the breasts
of bestial Marj
for the strong men
who

sleep between the legs of Lil

xxvii.

her
flesh
Came
at

meassandca V
         ingint
                 oA
chute
    i had cement for her,
    merrily
we became each
other humped to tumbling

garble   when
a
minute
pulled the sluice

        emerging.

concrete

xxviii.

raise the shade
will youse dearie?
rain
wouldn't that

get yer goat but
we don't care do
we dearie we should
worry about the rain

huh
dearie?
yknow
i'm

sorry for awl the
poor girls that
gets up god
knows when every

day of their
lives
aint you,
        oo-oo.   dearie

not so
hard dear

you're killing me

xi.

i am going to utter a tree,Nobody
shall stop me

but first
earth   ,the reckless oral darkness
raging with thin impulse

i will have

a
   dream
   i
   think it shall be roses and
spring will bring her
worms rushing through loam.

(afterward i'll
climb
by tall careful muscles

into nervous and accurate silence....But   first

you)

press easily
at first,it will be leaves
and a little harder

for roses
only a little harder

last   we
on the groaning flame of neat huge
trudging kiss moistly climbing hideously with
large
minute
hips,O

          .press

worms rushing slowly through loam

viii.

irreproachable ladies firmly lewd
on dangerous slabs of tilting din whose
mouths distinctly walk

                    your smiles accuse

the dusk with an untimid svelte subdued
magic

       while in your eyes there lives
a green egyptian noise. ladies with whom time

feeds especially his immense lips

On whose deep nakedness death most believes,
perpetual girls marching to love

whose bodies kiss me with the square crime
of life. . . . Cecile,the oval shove
of hiding pleasure.   Alice,stinging quips
of flesh.   Loretta, cut the comedy
kid....

    Fran Mag Glad Dorothy

ix.

nearer:breath of my breath:take not thy tingling
limbs from me:make my pain their crazy meal
letting thy tigers of smooth sweetness steal
slowly in dumb blossoms of new mingling:
deeper:blood of my blood:with upwardcringing
swiftness plunge these leopards of white dream
in the glad flesh of my fear:more neatly ream
this pith of darkness:carve an evilfringing
flower of madness on gritted lips
and on sprawled eyes squirming with light insane
chisel the killing flame that dizzily grips.

Querying greys between mouthed houses curl

thirstily.   Dead stars stink.   dawn.   Inane,

the poetic carcass of a girl

god pity me whom(god distinctly has)
the weightless svelte drifting sexual feather
of your shall i say body?follows
truly through a dribbling moan of jazz

whose arched occasional steep youth swallows
curvingly the keenness of my hips;
or,your first twitch of crisp boy flesh dips
my height in a firm fragile stinging weather,

(breathless with sharp necessary lips)kid

female cracksman of the nifty,ruffian-rogue,
laughing body with wise breasts half-grown,
lisping flesh quick to thread the fattish drone
of I Want a Doll,
                    wispish-agile feet with slid
steps parting the tousle of saxophonic brogue.

xvi.

twentyseven bums give a prostitute the once
-over. fiftythree(and one would see if it could)

eyes say the breasts look very good:
firmlysquirmy with a slight jounce,

thirteen pants have a hunch

admit in threedimensional distress
these hips were made for Horizontal Business
(set on big legs nice to pinch

assiduously which justgraze
each other).   As the lady lazily struts
                                        (her
thickish flesh superior to the genuine daze
of unmarketable excitation,

whose careless movements carefully scatter

pink propaganda of annihilation

xviii.

whereas by dark really released,the modern
flame of her indomitable body
uses a careful fierceness.   Her lips study
my head gripping for a decision:burn
the terrific fingers which grapple and joke
on my passionate anatomy
oh yes!   Large legs pinch,toes choke—
hair-thin strands of magic agony
....by day this lady in her limousine

oozes in fashionable traffic,just
a halfsmile (for society's sweet sake)
in the not too frail lips almost discussed;
between her and ourselves a nearly-opaque
perfume disinterestedly obscene.

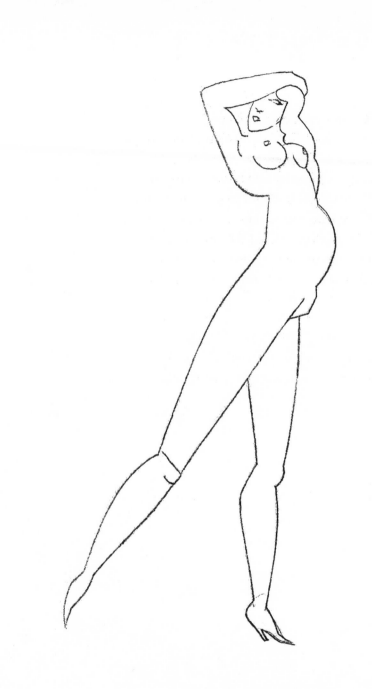

my girl's tall with hard long eyes
as she stands,with her long hard hands keeping
silence on her dress,good for sleeping
is her long hard body filled with surprise
like a white shocking wire,when she smiles
a hard long smile it sometimes makes
gaily go clean through me tickling aches,
and the weak noise of her eyes easily files
my impatience to an edge—my girl's tall
and taut,with thin legs just like a vine
that's spent all of its life on a garden-wall,
and is going to die.   When we grimly go to bed
with these legs she begins to heave and twine
about me,and to kiss my face and head.

xxi.

life boosts herself rapidly at me

through sagging debris of exploded day
the hulking perpendicular mammal
                                        a
grim epitome of chuckling flesh.
Weak thirsty fists of idiot futures bash

the bragging breasts,
                        puppy-faces to mouth
her ugly nipples squirming in pretty wrath,
gums skidding on slippery udders

                                she
lifts an impertinent puerperal face
and with astute fatuous swallowed eyes
smiles,
            one grin very distinctly wobbles
from the thinning lips me hugely which embrace.
as in the hairy notching of clenched thighs

a friendless dingy female frenzy bubbles

xiv.

the ivory performing rose

of you,worn upon my mind
all night,quitting only in the unkind

dawn its muscle amorous

pricks with minute odour these gross
days
        when i think of you and do not live:
and the empty twilight cannot grieve
nor the autumn,as i grieve,faint for your face

O stay with me slightly.   or until

with neat obscure obvious hands

Time stuff the sincere stomach of each mill

of the ingenious gods.(i am punished.
They have stolen into recent lands
the flower
                with their enormous fingers unwished

my naked lady framed
in twilight is an accident

whose niceness betters easily the intent
of genius—
                painting wholly feels ashamed
before this music,and poetry cannot
go near because perfectly fearful.

meanwhile these speak her wonderful
But i(having in my arms caught

the picture)hurry it slowly

to my mouth,taste the accurate demure
ferocious
        rhythm of
                precise
laziness.   Eat the price

of an imaginable gesture

exact warm unholy

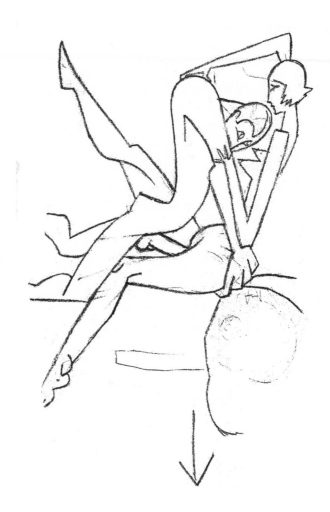

xx.

you asked me to come:it was raining a little,
and the spring;a clumsy brightness of air
wonderfully stumbled above the square,
little amorous-tadpole people wiggled

battered by stuttering pearl,
                              leaves jiggled
to the jigging fragrance of newness
—and then.   My crazy fingers liked your dress
....your kiss,your kiss was a distinct brittle

flower,and the flesh crisp set
my love-tooth on edge.   So until light
each having each we promised to forget—

wherefore is there nothing left to guess:
the cheap intelligent thighs,the electric trite
thighs;the hair stupidly priceless.

utterly and amusingly i am pash
possibly because
                              .dusk and if it
perhaps drea-mingly Is(not-
quite trees hugging with the rash,
coherent light
)only to trace with
stiffening slow shrill eyes beyond a fit-
and-cling of stuffs the alert willing myth
of body,which will make oddly to strut
my indolent priceless smile,
                              until
this very frail enormous star(do you see
it?)and this shall dance upon the nude
and final silence and shall the
(i do but touch you)timid lewd
moon plunge skilfully into the hill.

and this day it was Spring....us
drew lewdly the murmurous minute clumsy
smelloftheworld.   We intricately
alive,cleaving the luminous stammer of bodies
(eagerly just not each other touch)seeking,some
street which easily tickles a brittle fuss
of fragile huge humanity....
                              Numb
thoughts,kicking in the rivers of our blood,miss
by how terrible inches speech—it
made you a little dizzy did the world's smell
(but i was thinking why the girl-and-bird
of you move....moves....and also,i'll admit—)

till,at the corner of Nothing and Something,we heard
a handorgan in twilight playing like hell

i.

O It's Nice To Get Up In,the slipshod mucous kiss
of her riant belly's fooling bore
—When The Sun Begins To(with a phrasing crease
of hot subliminal lips,as if a score
of youngest angels suddenly should stretch neat necks
just to see how always squirms
the skilful mystery of Hell)me suddenly

grips in chuckles of supreme sex.

In The Good Old Summer Time.
My gorgeous bullet in tickling intuitive flight
aches,just,simply,into,her.   Thirsty
stirring.   (Must be summer.   Hush.   Worms.)
But It's Nicer To Lie In Bed
                    —eh?   I'm

not.   Again.   Hush.   God.   Please hold.   Tight

my strength becoming wistful in a glib

girl i consider her as a leaf
                                    thinks
of the sky,my mind takes to nib
-bling,of her posture.   (As an eye winks).

and almost i refrain from jumbling her
flesh whose casual mouth's coy rooting
dies also.   (my loveFist in her knuckling

thighs,
          with a sharp indecent stir
unclenches

               into fingers. . . . she too is tired.
Not of me.   The eyes which biggish loll

the hands' will tumbling into shall

—and Love 's a coach with gilt hopeless wheels mired
where sits rigidly her body's doll
gay exactly perishing sexual,

iii.

the dirty colours of her kiss have just
throttled
      my seeing blood,her heart's chatter

riveted a weeping skyscraper

in me

    i bite on the eyes' brittle crust
(only feeling the belly's merry thrust
Boost my huge passion like a business

and the Y her legs panting as they press

proffers its omelet of fluffy lust)
at six exactly
      the alarm tore

two slits in her cheeks.   A brain peered at the dawn.
she got up

      with a gashing yellow yawn
and tottered to a glass bumping things.
she picked wearily something from the floor

Her hair was mussed,and she coughed while tying strings

viii.

her careful distinct sex whose sharp lips comb

my mumbling gropeofstrength(staggered by the lug
of love)
            sincerely greets,with an occult shrug
asking Through her Muteness will slowly roam
my dumbNess?

                    her other,wet,warm

lips limp,across my bruising smile;
as rapidly upon the jiggled norm

of agony my grunting eyes pin tailored flames
Her being at this instant commits

an impenetrable transparency.
the harsh erecting breasts and uttering tits
punish my hug
                    presto!

                        the bright rile
of jovial hair extremely frames

the face in a hoop of grim ecstasy

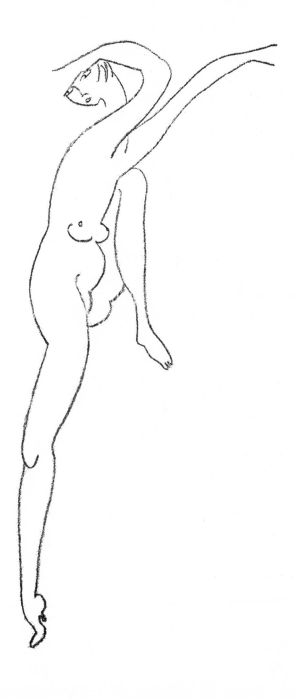

ix.

in making Marjorie god hurried
a boy's body on unsuspicious
legs of girl. his left hand quarried
the quartzlike face. his right slapped
the amusing big vital vicious
vegetable of her mouth.
Upon the whole he suddenly clapped
a tiny sunset of vermouth
-colour.   Hair. he put between
her lips a moist mistake,whose fragrance hurls
me into tears,as the dusty new-
ness of her obsolete gaze begins to.   lean....
a little against me,when for two
dollars i fill her hips with boys and girls

ii.

when i have thought of you somewhat too
much and am become perfectly and
simply Lustful....sense a gradual stir
of beginning muscle,and what it will do
to me before shutting....understand
i love you....feel your suddenly body reach
for me with a speed of white speech

(the simple instant of perfect hunger
Yes)
        how beautifully swims
the fooling world in my huge blood,
cracking brains A swiftlyenormous light
—and furiously puzzling through,prismatic,whims,
the chattering self perceives with hysterical fright

a comic tadpole wriggling in delicious mud

vi.

when you went away it was morning
(that is,big horses;light feeling up
streets;heels taking derbies (where?) a pup
hurriedly hunched over swill;one butting

trolley imposingly empty;snickering
shop doors unlocked by white-grub
faces) clothes in delicate hubbub

as you stood thinking of anything,

maybe the world....But i have wondered since
isn't it odd of you really to lie
a sharp agreeable flower between my

amused legs
                    kissing with little dints

of april,making the obscene shy
breasts tickle,laughing when i wilt and wince

vii.

i like my body when it is with your
body.   It is so quite new a thing.
Muscles better and nerves more.
i like your body.   i like what it does,
i like its hows.   i like to feel the spine
of your body and its bones,and the trembling
-firm-smooth ness and which i will
again and again and again
kiss,   i like kissing this and that of you,
i like,slowly stroking the,shocking fuzz
of your electric fur,and what-is-it comes
over parting flesh....And eyes big love-crumbs,

and possibly i like the thrill

of under me you so quite new

xix.

she being Brand

-new;and you
know consequently a
little stiff i was
careful of her and(having

thoroughly oiled the universal
joint tested my gas felt of
her radiator made sure her springs were O.

K.)i went right to it flooded-the-carburetor cranked her

up,slipped the
clutch(and then somehow got into reverse she
kicked what
the hell)next
minute i was back in neutral tried and

again slo-wly;bare,ly nudg.   ing(my

lev-er Right-
oh and her gears being in
A 1 shape passed
from low through
second-in-to-high like
greasedlightning)just as we turned the corner of Divinity

avenue i touched the accelerator and give

her the juice,good

        (it

was the first ride and believe i we was
happy to see how nice she acted right up to
the last minute coming back down by the Public
Gardens i slammed on

the
internalexpanding
&
externalcontracting
brakes Bothatonce and

brought allofher tremB
-ling
to a:dead.

stand-
;Still)

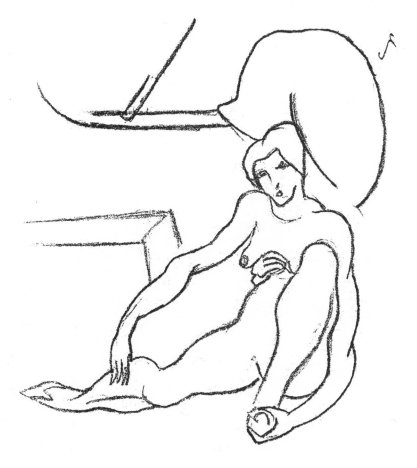

XXX.

(ponder,darling,these busted statues
of yon motheaten forum be aware
notice what hath remained
—the stone cringes
clinging to the stone,how obsolete

lips utter their extant smile....
remark

a few deleted of texture
or meaning monuments and dolls

resist Them Greediest Paws of careful
time all of which is extremely
unimportant)whereas Life

matters if or

when the your- and my-
idle vertical worthless
self unite in a peculiarly
momentary

partnership(to instigate
constructive

          Horizontal

business....even so,let us make haste
—consider well this ruined aqueduct

lady,
which used to lead something into somewhere)

may i feel said he
(i'll squeal said she
just once said he)
it's fun said she

(may i touch said he
how much said she
a lot said he)
why not said she

(let's go said he
not too far said she
what's too far said he
where you are said she)

may i stay said he
(which way said she
like this said he
if you kiss said she

may i move said he
is it love said she)
if you're willing said he
(but you're killing said she

but it's life said he
but your wife said she
now said he)
ow said she

(tiptop said he
don't stop said she
oh no said he)
go slow said she

(cccome? said he
ummm said she)
you're divine! said he
(you are Mine said she)

72.

wild(at our first)beasts uttered human words
—our second coming made stones sing like birds—
but o the starhushed silence which our third's

iv.

What is thy mouth to me?
A cup of sorrowful incense,
A tree of keen leaves,
An eager high ship,
A quiver of superb arrows.

What is thy breast to me?
A flower of new prayer,
A poem of firm light,
A well of cool birds,
A drawn bow trembling.

What is thy body to me?
A theatre of perfect silence,
A chariot of red speed;
And O, the dim feet
Of white-maned desires!

vii.

After your poppied hair inaugurates
Twilight, with earnest of what pleading pearls;
After the carnal vine your beauty curls
Upon me, with such tingling opiates
As immobile my literal flesh awaits;
Ere the attent wind spiritual whirls
Upward the murdered throstles and the merles
Of that prompt forest which your smile creates;

Pausing, I lift my eyes as best I can,
Where twain frail candles close their single arc
Upon a water-colour by Cézanne.
But you, love thirsty, breathe across the gleam;
For total terror of the actual dark
Changing the shy equivalents of dream.

ix.

When thou art dead,dead,and far from the splendid sin,
And the fleshless soul whines at the steep of the last abyss
To leave forever its heart acold in an earthy bed,

When,forth of the body which loved my body,the soul-within
Comes,naked from the pitiless metamorphosis,
What shall it say to mine,when we are dead,dead?

(When I am dead,dead, and they have laid thee in,
The body my lips so loved given to worms to kiss,
And the cool smooth throat,and bright hair of the head—).

iii.

my deathly body's deadly lady

smoothly-foolish exquisitely,tooled
(becoming exactly passionate Gladly

grips with chuckles of supreme sex

my mute-articulate protrusion)
Inviting my gorgeous bullet to vex

the fooling groove intuitive...

And the sharp ripples-of-her-brain bite
fondly into mine,
                    as the slow give-

of-hot-flesh Takes,me;in crazier waves of light
sweetsmelling
                    fragrant:
                                   unspeakable chips
Hacked,
          from the immense sun(whose day is drooled
on night—)and the abrupt ship-of-her lips

disintegrates,with a coy!explosion

iv.

first she like a piece of ill-oiled
machinery does a few naked tricks

next into unwhiteness,clumsily
lustful,plunges—covering the soiled
pillows with her violent hair
(eagerly then the huge greedily

Bed swallows easily our antics,
like smooth deep sweet ooze where
two guns lie,smile,grunting.)

"C'est la guerre"i probably suppose,
c'est la guerre busily hunting
for the valve which will stop this.
as i push aside roughly her nose

Hearing the large mouth mutter kiss pleece

vii.

as
we lie side by side
my little breasts become two sharp delightful strutting towers and
i shove hotly the lovingness of my belly against you

your arms are
young;
your arms will convince me,in the complete silence speaking
upon my body
their ultimate slender language.

do not laugh at my thighs.

there is between my big legs a crisp city.
when you touch me
it is Spring in the city;the streets beautifully writhe,
it is for you;do not frighten them,
all the houses terribly tighten
upon your coming:
and they are glad
as you fill the streets of my city with children.

my love you are a bright mountain which feels.
you are a keen mountain and an eager island whose
lively slopes are based always in the me which is shrugging,which is
under you and around you and forever:i am the hugging sea.

O mountain you cannot escape me
your roots are anchored in my silence;therefore O mountain
skilfully murder my breasts,still and always

i will hug you solemnly into me.

viii.

my lady is an ivory garden,
who is filled with flowers.

under the silent and great blossom
of subtle colour which is her hair
her ear is a frail and mysterious flower
her nostrils
are timid and exquisite
flowers skilfully moving
with the least caress of breathing,her
eyes and her mouth are three flowers.   My lady

is an ivory garden
her shoulders are smooth and shining
flowers
beneath which are the sharp and new
flowers of her little breasts tilting upward with love
her hand is five flowers
upon her whitest belly there is a clever dreamshaped flower
and her wrists are the merest most wonderful flowers   my

lady is filled
with flowers
her feet are slenderest
each is five flowers her ankle
is a minute flower
my lady's knees are two flowers

Her thighs are huge and firm flowers of night
and perfectly between
them eagerly sleeping
is

the sudden flower of complete amazement

my lady who is filled with flowers
is an ivory garden.

And the moon is a young man

who i see regularly,about twilight,
enter the garden smiling to
himself.

viii.

sometimes i am alive because with
me her alert treelike body sleeps
which i will feel slowly sharpening
becoming distinct with love slowly,
who in my shoulder sinks sweetly teeth
until we shall attain the Springsmelling
intense large togethercoloured instant

the moment pleasantly frightful

when,her mouth suddenly rising,wholly
begins with mine fiercely to fool
(and from my thighs which shrug and pant
a murdering rain leapingly reaches the
upward singular deepest flower which she
carries in a gesture of her hips)

ix.

o my wholly unwise and definite
lady of the wistful dollish hands

(whose nudity hurriedly extends
its final gesture lewd and exquisite,
with a certain agreeable and wee
decorum)o my wholly made for loving
lady
      (and what is left of me
your kissing breasts timidly complicate)

only always your kiss will grasp me quite.

Always only my arms completely press
through the hideous and bright night
your crazed and interesting nakedness

—from you always i only rise from something

slovenly beautiful gestureless

x.

my youthful lady will have other lovers
yet none with hearts more motionless than i
when to my lust she pleasantly uncovers
the thrilling hunger of her possible body.

Noone can be whose arms more hugely cry
whose lips more singularly starve to press her—
noone shall ever do unto my lady
what my blood does,when i hold and kiss her

(or if sometime she nakedly invite
me all her nakedness deeply to win
her flesh is like all the 'cellos of night
against the morning's single violin)

more far a thing than ships or flowers tell us,
her kiss furiously me understands
like a bright forest of fleet and huge trees
—then what if she shall have an hundred fellows?

she will remember,as i think,my hands

(it were not well to be in this thing jealous.)
My youthful lust will have no further ladies.

xiii.

you said Is
there anything which
is dead or alive more beautiful
than my body,to have in your fingers
(trembling ever so little)?
      Looking into
your eyes Nothing,i said,except the
air of spring smelling of never and forever.

....and through the lattice which moved as
if a hand is touched by a
hand(which
moved as though
fingers touch a girl's
breast,
lightly)
   Do you believe in always,the wind
said to the rain
I am too busy with
my flowers to believe,the rain answered

xiv.

is
it

because there struts a distinct silver lady

(we being passionate O yes)upon
the carpet of evening which thrills
with the minuteness of her
walking,for she walks

upon the evening
                        shy and luxurious   .and because

we
being

passionate perceive o Yes where(immensely
near)
simply,

.but with a colour like the ending of the world
rises

        slow
            ly

balloonlike

       the huge foetus of The Moon   ?

—with our gestures we pry
and our mouths battle into distinctness.   It
is this kiss which builds in us ever so softly

the coarse and terrible structure of the night.

xvii.

Lady,i will touch you with my mind.
Touch you and touch and touch
until you give
me suddenly a smile,shyly obscene

(lady i will
touch you with my mind.)Touch
you,that is all,

lightly and you utterly will become
with infinite ease

the poem which i do not write.

2.

Lady,since your footstep
is more frail than everything
which lives,than everything which breathes
in the earth and in the sea
because your body is more new,

a dream(skilfully who mimics,entirely who pictures
yourself a skilfully and entirely moving dream
with fingers,a dream with lifted little breasts
and with feet)touches

me through the day scarcely,timidly;

whereas,beside me through the long night and upon
me,always i feel the crisply and deeply moving
you which is so glad to be alive—

the you with hot big inward stealing
thighs,perfectly who steal me;or as the wise

sea steals entirely and skilfully the ignorant earth.

2.

in hammamet did camping queers et al)
with caverns measureless to man and how
lest which your worships deem apocryphal
o get a load of yonder arab now

bowed by the gaze of pederasts he queens
upon his toe and minces at the sand
the sorrows of young werther in his teens
and in his pants the urging of the hand

near and more near their draping selves redrape
lascivious hips against insisting sky
can there be no asylum no escape?
(his donkey looks mohammed in the eye

6.

"she had that softness which is falsity"
he frowned "plus budding strictly chasms of
uninnocence for eyes:and slippery
a pseudomind,not quite which could believe

in anything except most far from so
itself(with deep roots hugging fear's sweet mud
she floated on a silly nonworld's how
precarious inexistence like some dead

provocatively person of a thing
mancurious and manicured)i gave
the wandering stem a vivid(being young)
yank;and then vanished.   Seeing which,you dove

and brought me to the surface' smiling "by
my dick,which since has served me handily"

9.

devil crept in eden wood
(grope me wonderful grope me good)
and he saw two humans roaming
—hear that tree agroaning

woman chewed and man he chewed
(open beautiful open good)
and their eyes were wet and shining
—feel that snake aclimbing

lord he called and angel stood
(poke me darling o poke me good)
with a big thick sword all flaming
—o my god i'm coming

5.

                she,straddling my lap,
hinges(wherewith I tongue each eager pap)
and,reaching down,by merely fingertips
the hungry Visitor steers to love's lips
Whom(justly as she now begins to sit,
almost by almost giving her sweet weight)
O,how those hot thighs juicily embrace!
and (instant by deep instant)as her face
watches,scarcely alive,that magic Feast
greedily disappearing least by least—
through what a dizzily palpitating host
(sharp inch by inch)swoons sternly my huge Guest!
until(quite when our touching bellies dream)
unvisibly love's furthest secrets rhyme.

6.

n w
O
h
S
LoW
h
myGODye
s s

7.

b
et
wee
n no
w dis
appear
ing mou
ntains a
re drifti
ng christi
an how swee
tliest bell
s and we'l
l be you'
ll be i'
ll be ?
? ther
efore
let'
s k
is
s

there are so many tictoc
clocks everywhere telling people
what toctic time it is for
tictic instance five toc minutes toc
past six tic

Spring is not regulated and does
not get out of order nor do
its hands a little jerking move
over numbers slowly

                       we do not
wind it up it has no weights
springs wheels inside of
its slender self no indeed dear
nothing of the kind.

(So,when kiss Spring comes
we'll kiss each kiss other on kiss the kiss
lips because tic clocks toc don't make
a toctic difference
to kisskiss you and to
kiss me)